First published in the United States of America in 1997 by Walker Publishing Company, Inc.

Published simultaneously in Canada by Thomas Allen & Son Canada, Limited, Markham, Ontario

Library of Congress Cataloging-in-Publication Data
Vieira, Linda.
Grand Canyon: a trail through time/Linda Vieira; illustrations by Christopher Canyon.
p. cm.
Includes index.
Summary: Describes the deep trench known as the Grand Canyon, found in the Grand Canyon National Park, and the activities of visitors to the park.
ISBN 0-8027-8625-1 (hc). —ISBN 0-8027-8627-8 (reinforced)
1. Grand Canyon (Ariz.)—Juvenile literature. 2. Trail riding—Arizona—Grand Canyon—Juvenile literature. [1. Grand Canyon (Ariz.)
2. Grand Canyon National Park (Ariz.) 3. National parks and reserves.] I. Canyon, Christopher, ill. II. Title.
F788.V54 1997
917.91'320453—dc21   97-156   CIP   AC

Design by Janice Noto-Helmers

Printed in Hong Kong

2 4 6 8 10 9 7 5 3 1

To my wonderful Nick, who gives me the
time and space to follow my dreams.
This one is just for you. —L. V.

Dedicated to Robert J. Pagels —C. C.

A predawn storm rumbles over Grand Canyon National Park. Cracks of lightning shatter the dark sky, flashing above an enormous plateau of peaks, valleys, and trenches where ancient mountains once stood. The deepest trench is called the Grand Canyon, one of the Seven Natural Wonders of the World.

Dawn comes, bringing daylight to spires and buttes standing like sentries on the plateau, worn down by weathering and erosion. Coyotes teach their pups to hunt for food in thick forests along the edges of the Canyon.

6

housands of visitors from all over the world have come to view the splendor of the Grand Canyon. In campgrounds and lodges near the north and south rims, they prepare for the day's activities.

8

The morning sun climbs above distant mountains, revealing cliffs hanging over the Colorado River at the bottom of the Grand Canyon. The river took almost six million years to carve the Canyon, creating a channel about one mile deep and more than 275 miles long. Wind and water wore down its steep sides, widening the chasm between the cliffs. A raven glides across the opening, making lazy circles over the river far below.

The sun chases away shadows on the craggy rocks thousands of feet below the rims. Pack mules begin a five-hour trip down to the deepest part of the Canyon. They follow each other along a twisted, ten-mile trail to the riverbed. Clouds of dust follow them as voices from the top fade away.

Canyon visitors along the trail peer with curiosity at symbols of people and animals that were painted on a boulder by Havasupai Indians long ago. Havasupai still live in the Canyon today, tending their flocks and farms in the summertime, hunting small game and gathering nuts and berries in the winter months.

As the sun moves higher in the sky,
smaller side canyons with rocks layered
like multicolored ribbons come into view.
Bighorn sheep walk easily along the steep
walls of the canyons, looking for food in
hidden pockets of soil. Wildflowers stand
around them in patches of
purple and pink.

The mules continue down the trail to the inner gorge. They carry their riders past layers of rock that display millions of years of the Earth's geologic history. A canyon wren looks for bits of brush to line its nest, hidden in a rocky crevice just off the trail. It searches for twigs and grasses up and down the Canyon walls, flying past fossils of fish teeth and seashells.

19

The noonday sun glistens on a hidden creek near a granary built into the Canyon wall by Anasazi Indians almost 1,000 years ago. Squirrels chase through the now-empty granary, where crops and plants had been stored for food and trade.

A lizard scurries off the trail. It climbs over fossils of prehistoric trilobites, embedded in layers of shale millions of years ago when the land was covered by a primeval sea. After the mules pass, the lizard creeps out from its hiding place to soak up the warmth of the sun.

23

The afternoon sun hangs low in the sky. A white-breasted nuthatch flies above beavertail cacti along the rocky banks of the Colorado River. Its song drifts over ancient pink, white, and gray rocks at the river's edge, the roots of mountains that stood there almost two billion years ago. The water tumbles over cascading rapids, while trout search for quieter streams in which to spawn.

A ringtail cat drinks from a slower side stream, watching for predators up and down the red rocks and along the river nearby. Laughter echoes from a bunkhouse, as weary riders and hikers share stories of their descent into the Canyon.

The endless cycles of eroding rock and
moving water carved the Grand Canyon
millions of years ago. Blustering wind
and pounding rain continue to widen it,
grinding down rocks that used to be
mountains and volcanoes. The rushing
Colorado River deepens this natural
wonder, dragging rocks and mud along its
path through ancient plains and lava flows.

The mules rest for the night in a corral near the river, awaiting tomorrow's seven-hour trip back up to the top. Weather and erosion make tiny changes every day in the rocky walls along the trail. Millions of years into the future, the same forces of nature will continue to reshape the Grand Canyon, digging even deeper into the history of our planet.

31

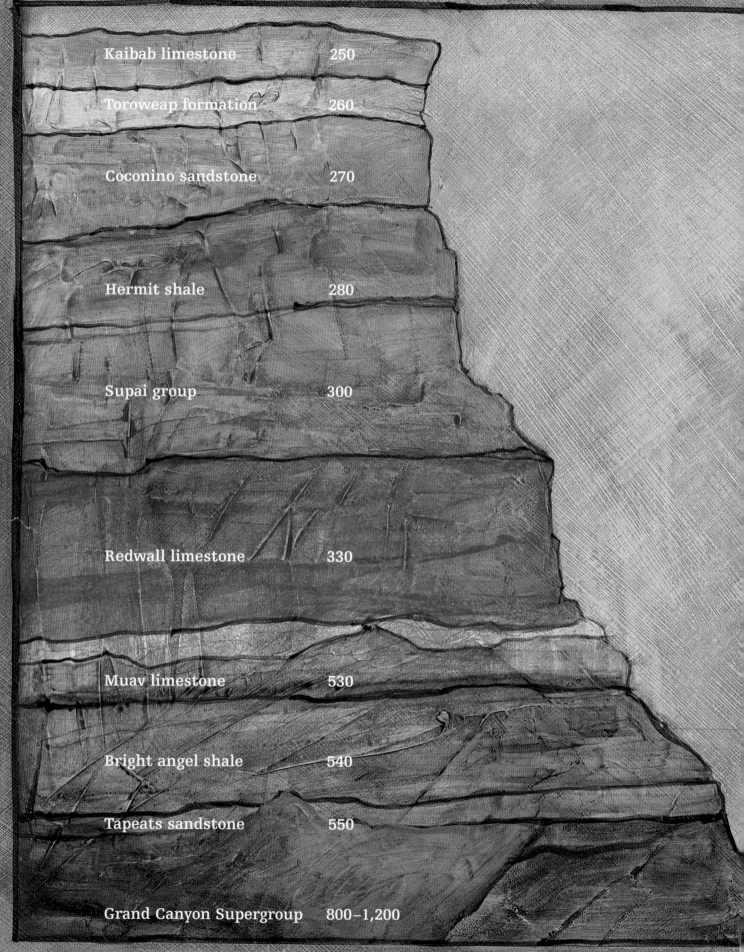

Rock name	Age (millions of years)
Kaibab limestone	250
Toroweap formation	260
Coconino sandstone	270
Hermit shale	280
Supai group	300
Redwall limestone	330
Muav limestone	530
Bright angel shale	540
Tapeats sandstone	550
Grand Canyon Supergroup	800–1,200